F. Baker

Traveller's Guide

A complete guide to the city of Washington and all places of note

surrounding

.

F. Baker

Traveller's Guide
A complete guide to the city of Washington and all places of note surrounding

ISBN/EAN: 9783337193430

Printed in Europe, USA, Canada, Australia, Japan

Cover: Foto ©Andreas Hilbeck / pixelio.de

More available books at **www.hansebooks.com**

Traveler's Guide.

THE TRAVELING PUBLIC

Will find in this book a complete

GUIDE TO THE CITY OF WASHINGTON

And all Places of Note Surrounding,

SUCH AS

ARLINGTON HEIGHTS,
MOUNT VERNON,
GEORGETOWN,
SOLDIERS' HOME, &c.

WILL ALSO FIND

The Arrival and Departure of Trains; the Time of Opening and Closing Mails; a Complete Description of and Access to all Public Buildings, Places of Worship, Secret Societies, and Places of Amusement; also, a Complete List of the most Prominent Merchants, Manufacturers, Legal Profession, Physicians, Artists, Fire and Life Insurance Cos., Patent Solicitors.

AND EVERY INFORMATION INTERESTING TO THE TRAVELER.

F. Baker, Publisher, No. 11 Wall Street, N.Y.

WASHINGTON, D. C.
GIBSON BROTHERS, PRINTERS, 271 PENNA. AVE.
1869.

POST OFFICE HOURS.

The Office is open from 6 A. M. to 9 o'clock P. M. except on Sunday, on which day it is open from 8 to 10 A. M. and 6 to 7 P. M.

The Money Order and Registered Letter Departments are open from 8 A. M. to 6 P. M. No business transacted in these departments on Sunday. The Letter Carriers' window is open from 7 to 9 o'clock P. M. General Delivery windows are open until 11 o'clock P. M.

••*

Time of Arrival and Closing of Mails.

Northern and Eastern Mails.
1st, due at 6.45 A. M.. closes 7 A. M.
2d, due at 5.40 P. M., closes 8 P. M.

Great Western and Baltimore Mails.
1st, due at 8.10 A. M.. closes 6 A. M.
2d, due at 9 A. M.
3d, due at 10.30 A. M.
4th, due at 6.30 P. M., closes 7 P. M.

Southern Mails, via Orange & Alexandria R. R., for Lynchburg, Chattanooga and New Orleans.
Due at 7.35 P. M., closes 6 A. M.

Southern Mails, via Richmond and Fredericksburg.
1st, due at 6.45 A. M., closes at 6 A. M.
2d, due at 7 P. M., closes 5.40 P. M.

Rockville, Maryland, Mail.
Due at 6 P. M., closes 6.30 P. M.

Annapolis Mail.
1st, due at 10.30 A. M., closes 12 M.
2d, due at 6.30 P. M., closes 6 A. M.

Alexandria, Va., Mail.
1st, due at 7 A. M., closes 5 A. M.
2d, due at 7.35 P. M., closes 5 P. M. -

Georgetown, D. C., Mail.
1st, due at 6.30 A. M, closes 7 A. M.
2d, due at 12.30 P. M., closes 1 P. M.
3d, due at 5.30 P. M., closes 7 P. M.

Norfolk, Va., Mail.
1st, due at 10.30 A. M.. closes 1.30 P. M.
2d, due at 5.40 P. M., closes 7.30 P. M.

Upper Marlboro', Md., Mail.
Due at 5 P. M., closes.6.30 A. M.

Piscataway and Duffield Mail.
Due Monday, Wednesday and Friday, at 7 P. M.; closes Tuesday, Thursday and Saturday, at 6 A. M.

Port Tobacco, Md., Mail.
Due 7 P. M., closes 6 A. M.

Leesburg, Va., Mail.
Due 6.30 P. M., closes 6 A. M.

Brookville, Md., Mail.
Due 10 A. M.. closes 1.30 P. M.
closes 7 A. M.

Sandy Spring, Md., Mail.
Due 10 A. M.. closes 7 P. M.

Mail for Eastern Shore of Maryland.
Due 10 A. M., closes 7 P. M.

On Sunday only one Mail is received from the North and two from the West. South and North-West. Mails departing on this day for these routes close at 7.30 P. M , including Norfolk, Old Point Comfort and Portsmouth.

MONEY ORDER OFFICE.

Especial attention is called to the Money Order System, as a safe and cheap method of transmitting small sums through the mails.

Orders are issued in sums not more than $50. Larger amounts can be sent to the same person at the same time by additional orders.

Rates as follows :
On Orders not exceeding $20, 10 cents.
Over $20 and not exceeding $30, 15 cents.
Over $40 and not exceeding $50, 25 cents.

Postage to Canada.
Postage on books and other printed matter, including newspapers, can only be paid to the Canada Line.
Books not exceeding 4 ozs. in weight, 4 cents; for each additional 4 ozs. or fraction 4 cents.

Unsealed Circulars.
Not exceeding three in number to one address, 2 cents; over three and not exceeding six to one address, 4 cents. Any large number the same proportionate rates.

Transcript Printed Matter.
One package to one address, not exceeding 4 ozs., 2 cents; and for each additional 4 ozs. or fraction thereof, 2 cents. No transcript printed matter is forwarded unless prepaid.

Guide to Washington.

We now propose to take the traveler to all the places of note in and about Washington, commencing with the most prominent building, which is the Capitol. This magnificent structure is situated at the intersection of Pennsylvania, New Jersey, and Maryland Avenues. This is a building of which the American people may well be proud. It is built in the five orders of architecture, with ten different kinds of marble, surmounted by a dome of solid iron. The entire length of the building, from the Senate Chamber, in the North, to the Hall of Representatives, in the South, is 850 feet. Its breadth, from East to West, is 500 feet: the Dome having a base diameter of 96 feet, and a clear height of 220 feet. The Dome presents a magnificent spectacle when illuminated with its thousand gas-lights, presenting to the eye its many historical paintings, designed and executed by the most eminent artists of the world. Having introduced you into this magnificent building, we would suggest that you procure a small guide, viz: a pamphlet which can be had in the Rotunda, (at a trifling cost,) containing a Key to the Senate Chamber and House of Representatives: also of everything of importance in and about the building.

From the Capitol proceed to the Smithsonian Institute, via 7th Street cars, to the East gate, where you will pass through grounds beautifully laid out and handsomely decorated. This is a department more particularly calculated to interest the antiquarian, but, nevertheless, any scientific mind will here find much to its edification. This Institution has recently lost many of its chief atractions by fire, consisting of ancient paintings, engravings, &c., which can never be replaced. Animals may here be seen ranging in size from the smallest insect to the largest and most gigantic kings of the

---

History of the War.

Although we might go many years back to find the first seeds of the rebellion, yet this record properly commences with the assembling of the South Carolina Convention at Columbia, on the 17th of December, 1860. The Southern leaders foreseeing the defeat of their measures by the election of Abraham Lincoln, issued manifestoes and made violent speeches, calculated to arouse the passions of the people. After the 6th of November, the Southerners prosecuted war measures energetically. Cabinet officers scattered the army and navy, and robbed the Federal Treasury. Many of the more moderate fought against secession for a long time, but were finally overwhelmed by the tide and carried with it: All efforts on the part of committees appointed by both Houses of Congress to harmonize the antagonistic elements were unsuccessful. On the 8th of November, the Palmetto flag was hoisted in Charleston, and South Carolina voted $100,000 to purchase arms. On the 10th a committee was called, and the United States officers in Charleston resigned. Georgia also voted $1,000,000 to arm the State. Major Anderson was placed in command at Fort Moultrie. President Buchanan took the position that the General Government had no authority to coerce a State if she withdrew from the Union. Louisiana at once appropriated $500,000 for military purposes. Howell Cobb, Secretary of the Treasury, resigned. President Buchanan opposed the reinforcement of the forts of Charleston harbor, and then Gen. Cass, Secretary of State, resigned in disgust. On the 20th South Carolina seceded by a unanimous vote in her convention, and the news was joyfully received throughout the South. One hundred guns were fired at New Orleans, and the Pelican flag unfurled. "The people," said the *Charleston Mercury*, "will obey the call for war, and take the forts." On the 24th Gov. Pickens, of South Carolina, declared that State "a free and independent State." On the 26th, Major Anderson evacuated Fort Moultrie and occupied Fort Sumter. The guns at Moultrie were spiked and the carriages destroyed. A secession meeting was held in

many enterprising explorers have met a like fate. Also among the curiosities are some of the largest meteoric formations that have ever visited us from the boundless realms of space, one of which weighs some twelve hundred pounds. Where and how these ponderous nuggets of iron were formed,

---

STRANGERS, NOTICE!

—o—

First Class and Fashionable Shoe Store!

—·—

ALWAYS ON HAND, FOR GENTLEMEN

Patent Leather Boots,
Congress and Low Shoes.

Box Toes and Plain French Calf Boots for Gents, $10.

ALSO, BOOTS MADE TO ORDER.

—·—

BOYS' BOOTS AND SHOES
Of all styles, and at prices that will satisfy the most economical.

—o—

Ladies', Ladies'

FRENCH KID BUTTON BOOTS, FRENCH LASTING BUTTON BOOTS,
CLOTH BUTTON BOOTS,
WHITE AND BRONZE BOOTS OF ALL STYLES.

Ladies, Misses and Children's Shoes of all makes, for house and all other wear.

In short, there is nothing in our line that cannot be had at once or by order.

GENTLEMEN'S SLIPPERS SOLED In First Class Style.

At GEO. B. WILSON & CO'S,
Late of 340 Pennsylvania Avenue,
Now 502 Seventh St., under Odd-Fellows' Hall, 2d block from Pa. Ave.

☞ A note addressed to our establishment will meet with prompt attention.

Richmond, Va., on the 27th. On the 28th, Gov. Hicks refused to convene the Legislature of Maryland. On the 29th, John B. Floyd, Secretary of War, resigned. 30th, South Carolina troops took possession of the Charleston arsenal, and strong fortifications were ordered to prevent communications with Major Anderson. January 1st, 1861—great excitement in Charleston, preparations being made to take Fort Sumter. Threatening letters were

YATES & WISWALL,

523 7th Street, bet. Market Space and D St.

WHOLESALE & RETAIL DEALERS IN

Foreign & Domestic Dry Goods

ALSO,

Gentlemen's

FURNISHING GOODS!

EVERY VARIETY OF

Ladies' Dress Goods of the Latest Patterns

AND AT

THE LOWEST PRICES.

Strangers in Washington will do well to give us a call before purchasing elsewhere, as our goods will bear comparison with any in the country.

ing. This is an institution of peculiar interest to the great mass of the American people, and is destined to occupy a very prominent position, although at present in its infancy, and a department that has received no considerable financial aid from Congress ; but, notwithstanding the obstacles it has had

---

N. P. CHIPMAN.   A. A. HOSMER.   CHARLES D. GILMORE.

CHIPMAN, HOSMER & CO.

No. 407 F Street, near Patent and Post Offices,

ATTORNEYS AT LAW,

Practice in the Supreme Court and Court of Claims; attend to all classes of cases arising under treaties.

Attorneys for the Collection of Claims.

We publish Pamphlets giving laws of Congress relative to Bounties, Pensions, Officers' Accounts, Claims in Land Office, Navy Bag Money, Prisoners of War, Back Pay, Prize Money, Naval Bounty, Transfers from Army to Navy, Additional pay to Officers for Servants: Officers commissioned, not mustered; Horses, Equipments, Mileage, Commutations: Delayed, Suspended, or Rejected Claims; Disbursing Officers, Property Purchased or Seized, Quartermaster's and Commissary Stores, Contractors' Claims, Compensations to Loyal Owners, Fees, Blanks and Forms, Claims in the South, and Patents.

These Pamphlets are valuable to Agents and the Profession, and will be sent to any one on application, without charge.

SOLICITORS OF PATENTS.

By reason of our favorable location and facilities here, we make matters pertaining to PATENTS a branch of our business, and for the advantage of Inventors, and others interested, devote the services of one of the most experienced and successful solicitors to the procurement of Letters Patent.

Rejected or abandoned cases of value particularly solicited. See our Pamphlet, &c.

INTERNAL REVENUE BUSINESS.

We have formed a special partnership with WILLIAM RICHARDS, Esq., late of the Internal Revenue Bureau, for the prosecution of all business arising under the Internal Revenue Laws and Regulations. Special attention given to Collectors' Accounts, Claims for Refunding, Distillery Cases, and Compromises.

LETTER FROM HON. E. A. ROLLINS, LATE COMMISSIONER OF INTERNAL REVENUE.

PHILADELPHIA, *July 9*, 1869.

MY DEAR SIR: I am very glad to learn of your associating yourself in business with Messrs. CHIPMAN, HOSMER & Co. Your long connection with the Internal Revenue service, and the important positions occupied by you from time to time in the Office of Commissioner, will enable you to transact business with facility, and the excellent reputation of Messrs. CHIPMAN, HOSMER & Co. cannot but insure a large business in the future. I am very truly yours.   E. A. ROLLINS.
WM. RICHARDS, Esq., *Washington, D. C.*

---

barrels of powder: Fort Moultrie occupied by Alabama troops: Fast day throughout the United States. 5th—Steamer *Star of the West* cleared at New York, supposed for Charleston. 6th—Great Union meeting in Chicago, Illinois. Fort Washington, on the Potomac, reinforced. Forty tons of powder, shot, and shell, sent South by Southern Express Agents. 7th—Senators Toombs and Wigfall arrested for treason: Alabama Convention

to surmount, the institution is prepared to-day to impart to the farmer information that can be had in no other way. We would introduce our visitor
to Prof. Glover, who may be found in the Museum, who will take pleasure
in explaining the objects and advantages of the Department.

organized. 8th Forts Casswell and Johnson occupied by North Caro-
linians; Jacob Thompson, Secretary of the Navy, resigned: Sub-Treasurer
at Charleston not allowed to pay out any more money. 9th Mississippi seceded; *Star of the West* fired upon by the Morris Island battery
when she attempted to enter Charleston harbor, and the act was sanctioned
by Gov. Pickens. 11th Florida and Alabama seceded. 19th Georgia se-

But few comparatively of the American people avail themselves of the advantages of this Department. The grounds surrounding this building are beautifully laid out, and planted with the choicest flowers from all parts of the world. The Museum, so called, is more properly speaking the Farmer's

ceded. 24th— U. S. arsenal at Augusta, Georgia, surrendered to the State. 26th— Louisiana seceded. 27th— Ex-Secretary Floyd indicted for conspiracy against the Government, and abstraction of bonds. 31st— $511,000 in Government funds were captured at New Orleans.

1861. February 1st— The secession of Texas submitted to the people. 5th— Peace convention organized at Washington. 8th— Jefferson Davis

Guide, and can be made to him of great value, as the institution is to the visitor a place of entertainment.

Still west of this Department is to be seen a huge pile of stones, and the visitor will wonder what this uncouth pile is intended for; but do not be

elected President, and Alex. H. Stevens, Vice President of the confederate States. 23d - Abraham Lincoln, President elect, arrived in Washington. March 4th He was inaugurated; Texas seceded same day. 9th The army of the confederate States established. April 11th—Fort Sumter summoned to surrender; Major Anderson, in command, refused. 12th The rebels opened fire from Fort Moultrie on Sumter; the conflict continued till the

surprised when we inform you that this is the far-famed Washington Monument—the column to commemorate the "Father of our Country." This is what the Monument Committee have given their constituents for the many dollars that have been dropped into the thousands of places of deposit that

JAS. FULLERTON,

Attorney and Counsellor at Law,

SOLICITOR OF PATENTS,

AND

GENERAL CLAIM AGENT,

409 F STREET, between 6th & 7th Streets, near the Patent and General Post Offices,

Post-Office Box 90,

WASHINGTON, D. C.

Personal attention given to all business before the Court of Claims and the various departments of Government.

Compensation procured for Vessels, Horses, Wagons, Mules, &c.

Lost or destroyed in the public service, and for services rendered ; also for

PROVISIONS, STOCK, WOOD, FORAGE, OR OTHER PROPERTY,

Appropriated for military purposes by officers of the Army or Navy.

PATENTS.

The inventor of any new and useful tool, device, or substance, or of any improvement or new application, is entitled to a patent securing the exclusive profit arising out of its use, manufacture, or sale. A written description of the new invention should be sent to Mr. FULLERTON, who will ascertain if it be patentable before advising the inventor to incur the expense of an application.

Mr. FULLERTON is well and favorably known in Washington City, where he has resided for many years, and, by faithful personal attention to the interests of his clients, and very moderate charges, has been very successful, heretofore, in giving satisfaction to his numerous correspondents in all sections of the country.

☞ He will at all times take pleasure in giving correspondents desired information when stamps are enclosed for return postage.

next day, when Major Anderson capitulated. 15th—Sumter evacuated ; President Lincoln called for 75,000 men for three months, and called an extra session of Congress to meet on the 4th of July. 16th—New York State appropriated $3,000,000. 17th—The Steamer *Star of the West* and cargo seized by the Texans. 18th—The Government buildings at Harper's Ferry destroyed. 19th A mob at Baltimore resist the militia on their way to

stare you in the face throughout the country. It was thought advisable that large sums should not be received from any one to defray the expenses of the Monument, as every American would wish to be represented among the contributors. But whether the American people are indifferent to the name

FOR THE BEST AND CHEAPEST
GENTS'
FURNISHING GOODS

Go To

FRANC & GOLDMAN,

458 Seventh St., opp. Patent Office,

AND

516 Seventh St., bet. D and E Sts.

WHERE THEY HAVE A

Larger Assortment and Lower Prices

THAN ANY OTHER ESTABLISHMENT IN THIS CITY.

Remember the Places.

FINE DRESS SHIRTS MADE TO ORDER.

Washington : President Lincoln declared a blockade of the Southern ports ; Philadelphia appropriated $1,000,000, and New York the same, for war purposes. 26th The capital declared now safely protected. 28th Maryland refused to secede. May 2d Connecticut appropriated $2,000,000 for military purposes. 13th Queen Victoria issued her proclamation of neutrality ; McClellan and Frémont appointed Major Generals in the regular

of Washington or the committee has pocketed the funds is not for us to say. But sure it is that the Monument, which was to be some six hundred feet high and surrounded by beautiful columns, altogether presenting a token of respect to the " Father of our Country," is an unsightly pile of stone, some

---

---

service. 17th— Harper's Ferry fortified by the rebels. 18th—Arkansas admitted into the Southern Confederacy. 20th—North Carolina seceded ; Jeff. Davis signed the repudiation act. 24th—Col. Ellsworth killed at the Marshall House, Alexandria, by Jas. Jackson, while attempting to remove from the roof a rebel flag. 27th—Mobile and Savannah blockaded. June 3d— Gen. Beauregard assumed command of the Confederate forces at Manassas

180 feet high, with nothing to mark it as a tribute to one so justly claiming the homage of his people.

In leaving the Monument grounds we pass up Fourteenth street to Pennsylvania avenue; thence to the Treasury Building. This is hardly second

Junction; Battle of Philippi, Va. 10th—Battle of Big Bethel; thirteen Union officers and men killed, thirty wounded; rebel loss unknown. 15th—Gen. Lyon entered Jefferson city. 18th—Balloon ascension for military purposes from Washington; President Lincoln received the first message ever sent from a balloon. 23d—Gen. McClellan assumed command in person of the forces in West Virginia. 27th—Gen. Frémont arrived in Boston from

to the Capitol in importance, as a place of interest to the visitor. It was here that the weapons of war were made - *greenbacks.* Here are kept the accounts of the army and navy ; the statistics of foreign commerce ; and from here is disbursed the money that pays all our foreign servants. This building alone

W. S. BAILEY'S

BOARDING HOUSE,

331 Pennsylvania Avenue,

Between 6th and 7th Sts.

GENTLEMEN OR LADIES

WITH OR WITHOUT FAMILIES,

WISHING PLEASANT AND WELL

FURNISHED ROOMS

WITH BOARD,

Will do well to call on me before looking elsewhere. Our location is not only central, but quiet and easy of access to and from all parts of the City.

Europe with a large quantity of arms. July 4th Congress met ; the President recommended the raising of 400,000 men and $400,000,000. 5th —Battle of Carthage, Mo.; Confederate loss estimated at from three to five hundred ; Union loss, thirteen killed and thirty-one wounded. 10th The Senate passed a bill authorizing the enlistment of 500,000 men, and voting $500,000,000 for the "suppression of the rebellion ;" Battle of Rich Moun-

employs some 3,000 clerks, both male and female, making an army nearly as large as Washington had to free his country from the iron grasp of Great Britain. This building is a monument to American architecture, and is calculated to stem the storm of many centuries.

T. C. THEAKER,

SOLICITOR OF PATENTS,

AND

Attorney in Patent Cases,

Office, Room No. 19, May Building, Cor. 7th & E Sts.

WASHINGTON, D. C.

Assisted in all branches of the Law of Patents by the law firm of

BARTLEY & STANTON.

WHOSE OFFICE IS IN THE SAME BUILDING, ROOMS NOS. 2 AND 4.

HAVING made Mechanics and Machinery my study and business for more than thirty years, and having had an experience of seven years in the Patent Office—four and a half years as Examiner-in-Chief, and two and a half years as United States Commissioner of Patents—and having secured the professional assistance of the eminent law firm of BARTLEY & STANTON in all matters relating to the Law of Patents, I offer my services to Inventors and Patentees, with the assurance that all cases entrusted to me shall be skilfully conducted, and receive prompt attention, in either the Patent Office or in the Courts.

T. C. THEAKER.

tain : Confederates defeated, losing all they had, with sixty killed and a large number wounded ; Rosecrans lost twenty killed and forty wounded. 17th Fight at Scareytown : the Unionists defeated. 20th Confederate Congress met at Richmond. 21st Battle of Bull Run : the Union forces engaged were about 20,000 : the rebels 40,000, with a reserve of 25,000 at Manassas Junction ; Unionists defeated with a loss of 2,708 ; rebel loss, 1,902. 22d Gen.

All visitors to Washington should not fail to visit Arlington. But few places will afford more profit to sight-seers. The scenery is most picturesque, overlooking, as it does, Washington, the Potomac river, and Alexandria in the distance. Arlington is famous as being the property of George Wash-

McClellan ordered to the command of the Army of the Potomac, succeeding Gen. McDowell ; Rosecrans appointed brigadier general of the regular army. 27th—Resolution approving the acts of President Lincoln submitted to the Senate by Senator Andrew Johnson. 31st—Gen. Scott ordered that the houses, tombs, and property at Mount Vernon should be respected under any and all circumstances. Aug. 3d—Confiscation act passed the House. 10th—

ington Parke Custis, which descended to his daughter Mary, wife of Robert E. Lee, who owned and occupied it for many years until the rebellion, when it was sold for taxes and bought by the Government, who now occupy it as a a resting-place for 16,000 brave men who died that their country might live.

HARVEY SPALDING,

Government Claims Attorney

Office, Room 11, Intelligencer Building,

SEVENTH STREET WEST,

WASHINGTON, D. C.

Makes Collections with all possible dispatch of Claims of every description against the Government, and in part as follows, viz:

Liquidation and Unliquidated Damages upon all express contracts not executed in full, or which have been violated by the United States, which cases cover services rendered and supplies and materials furnished in every department of the Government; also, supplies and materials taken by competent authority since the late war without contract or agreement in respect to the same; also classes of the latter cases arising during the war, which by law are not regarded as appropriations, by virtue of the belligerent right of the Government. Also, Bounties, Pensions, Property of all classes lost in the military service, and all other cases founded on existing laws.

Claims of Loyal Citizens of Southern States arising during the war can now be collected only by application to Congress, but it is to be hoped that a general law will soon be enacted whereby such claims may be settled.

I make a specialty of Rejected and Litigated Cases, and will give, upon application, references as to numerous such cases in which I have been successful.

In Claims entrusted to my care, I undertake to demonstrate that the policy which is declared and confirmed, of full payment of the funded and currency debt, applies also to other debts of the United States.

Battle of Wilson's Creek ; Union victory, with loss of 1,235 killed, wounded and missing ; that of the rebels 1,300. 14th—Martial law declared in St. Louis by Gen. Frémont. 19th—Missouri seceded. 30th—The whole State of Missouri declared under martial law by Gen. Frémont. Sept. 6th—Gen. Grant took possession of Paducah, Ky., with two regiments, in the face of a rebel force of 4,000 men. 11th—President Lincoln modified Gen. Frémont's

To visit Arlington the visitor will take private conveyance, as there is no other. The route lays through Georgetown, passing over the Aqueduct bridge, taking the road to the left one and a half miles, which brings you to the front of the old mansion. The building is old style, with immense

---

T. J. THOMPSON,

Watch and Clock Maker

257 F Street, near Ebbitt House,

Between 13th and 14th Sts.

WATCHES, CLOCKS, AND JEWELRY

REPAIRED.

Particular attention given to Repairing

CHRONOMETER, LEVER DUPLEX

AND OTHER FINE WATCHES.

---

emancipation proclamation. 20th—Col. Mulligan was forced, for want of water and supplies, to surrender Lexington to the rebel general, Price, after offering to meet him in open field, four to one, which Price declined. 29th— Two regiments from Pennsylvania, mistaking each other for rebels, fired into each other, and 9 men were killed, and 25, including 3 officers, were wounded before the mistake was discovered. Oct. 3d—Gen. Frémont removed, which

columns in front, and elevated as it is on so beautiful a mound, presents altogether a grand appearance. The old building is unoccupied otherwise than as an office. The east room is fitted up as a greenhouse, and contains many rare plants of which the ladies are so fond.

U. S. and European

PATENT AGENCY.

KNIGHT BROTHERS,

406 F STREET,

Five doors east of United States Patent Office.

OCTAVIUS KNIGHT having resigned the position held by him from 1860 to 1867 as Superintendent of Munn & Co's Scientific American Patent Agency, offers his personal services to all who intend to apply for Letters Patent, or have Pending or Rejected Applications, or other business before the Patent Office. His large experience in conducting applications to a successful issue will give assurance of his ability to act with dispatch and success.

Special attention given to the prosecution of **INTERFERENCES, EXTENSIONS,** and **REJECTED APPLICATIONS,** and **REISSUING DEFECTIVE PATENTS.**

Inventions possessing practical merit can be made very profitable if patented abroad. Our arrangements for securing patents in all foreign countries where patents are granted are of the most complete and efficient character.

All communications strictly confidential.

REFERENCES:

Hon. S. P. Chase, Chief Justice of U. S.   Hon. H. Stanbery, late Att'y Gen'l, U. S.
" S. S. Fisher, Commissioner of Patents.   " S. C. Pomeroy, U. S. S.
Prof. Jos. Henry, Sec'y Smithsonian Institute.   " Wm. Lawrence, M. C.
Hon. S. S. Marshall, M. C.

caused great excitement in St. Louis. 21st—Battle of Fredericktown, Mo.: Union victory by a loss of 6 killed and 40 wounded ; rebel loss, Gen. Lowe was killed and 200 others, and a large number wounded. 24th—Mason and Slidell formally received at Havana ; the writ of *habeas corpus* suspended in the District of Columbia. Nov. 1st—Gen. Scott's name placed on the retired list of officers of the army ; Major General Geo. B. McClellan succeeded him

The visitor will be well pleased by a drive up the river as far as the Great Falls, passing on his way the Chain bridge and Little Falls, a distance of 18 miles. The scenery along the Potomac is grand and beautiful. The Acqueduct bridge is also well worth a visit, as it is said to be the most gigantic

as General-in-chief of the army. 7th—Battle of Belmont; Union loss, 84 killed, 288 wounded, and 235 prisoners; Confederate loss, 261 killed, 427 wounded, and 278 prisoners; Bombardment of Port Royal; Beaufort, and Hilton Head occupied by the Union troops; 10th—Gen. Halleck placed in command of the Department of the West. 18th—Confederate Congress met at Richmond. 25th—General Lee declared Charleston under martial law;

piece of stone-masonry work in the world. Over this bridge the water is brought to Washington city. The Soldiers' Home is also worth a visit. Although a one-legged cripple in itself is not calculated to afford much pleasure to the visitor, yet the pleasant spot on which the Home is situated

---

GEORGE W. HARVEY
SUCCESSOR TO HARVEY & CO.

UNDERTAKER

410 Seventh Street,

BETWEEN G AND H STREETS,

WASHINGTON, D. C.

---

specie payment suspended in Louisiana. December, 1861 Southern papers rejoicing at the prospect of a war between England and the United States. 23d Forty-seven Unionists routed one hundred and eighteen confederates in Perry co., Ky., and wounded eighteen. January 1, 1862 Battle on Port Royal Island; Unionists victorious; Fort Pickens opened fire on the confederate forts at Pensacola; Fort Barrancas was breached; Warrington was

and the fine view from thence will amply compensate for the trouble taken to reach it. As there are no cars running to this place, it will be necessary to take a private conveyance and go up either Seventh or Fourteenth street, as it is situated on the hill between the extreme end of both. The Howard

---

---

burned; Mason and Slidell left Fort Warren for Europe. 13th—Simon Cameron, Secretary of War, resigned; Edwin M. Stanton was appointed to succeed him. 19th -Battle of Mill Spring: the first of a series of brilliant Union victories in the West. Feb. 6th—Bombardment of Fort Henry. 8th Battle of Roanoke Island. 14th—Battle of Fort Donelson. March 6th Battle of Pea Ridge. 23d Battle of Winchester. 24th Bombardment of

ALEXANDER & MASON,

SOLICITORS OF

AMERICAN AND EUROPEAN

PATENTS

AND

Counsellors at Patent Law,

FIFTEEN YEARS' EXPERIENCE.

460 Seventh Street,

OPPOSITE U. S. PATENT OFFICE,

WASHINGTON, D. C.

☞ PATENTS secured on more reasonable terms and in shorter time than through any other Agency in the United States.

ALEXANDER
AND
MASON.

SOLICITORS
OF
AMERICAN PATENTS AND COUNSELLORS AT PATENT
AND
EUROPEAN LAW

No 460
7TH ST
RE ISSUE
PATENT OFFICE
WASHINGTON, D.C.

University (or Freedman's Bureau) is also situated near by, at the terminus of the Seventh-street cars.   To visit Alexandria from any point in the vicinity of Pennsylvania avenue, take the cars on said avenue, and take a check at their junction with Seventh street and go south to the Ferry : here take the

---

steamboat, and a pleasant ride of some fifteen minutes will land you at the foot of this old and venerable city. It will be remembered that the Marshall House, in this city, was the place where the noble Colonel Ellsworth fell by the hand of the landlord, James Jackson, as the first martyr of the rebellion.

JIRDINSTON & BOUVET,

Dealers in Fine Groceries

175

Penna. Avenue, bet. 17th and 18th Sts.

FINE TEAS,

Choice Wines and Liquors

FOR FAMILY USE KEPT CONSTANTLY ON HAND.

ALSO EVERY ASSORTMENT OF

Foreign and Domestic Fruits.

GOODS SENT TO ANY PART OF THE CITY FREE OF CHARGE.

Battle of Cedar Mountain. 30th—Second battle of Bull Run. September 2—General McClellan placed in command of the defences of Washington. September 17th—Battle of Antietam; 100,000 men engaged on each side: Union victory with a loss of over 2,000 killed, 9,416 wounded, and 1,000 missing; confederate loss 14,000. October 3d—Commencement of the battles at Corinth. November 5, 1862—General McClellan relieved of the com-

26

WILLIAM C. LYCETT,

Book-Binder & Paper Ruler,

271 Pennsylvania Avenue,

SOUTH SIDE—NEAR ELEVENTH STREET.

Gibson Brothers, Printers,

271, SOUTH SIDE PENNSYLVANIA AVENUE,

WASHINGTON, D. C.

At the junction, as before said, of Seventh street and Pennsylvania avenue cars the conductor will give you a check either to Georgetown or the Navy Yard. The cars running on F street give no transfer tickets; they charge seven cents, and require the passenger to put the ticket or money into the

---

SAMUEL HARRIS,

MANUFACTURER OF

Harris' Patent Engine

WARRANTED

EQUAL TO PISTON ENGINES,

AND

SOLD AT ONE-HALF THE PRICE.

...

Machinist and Model Maker.

SPECIAL ATTENTION PAID TO

Repairing Printing Presses, Mill Work, Sewing Machines, &c.

CALL AND EXAMINE

THE ENGINE AT WORK AT THE SHOP.

SOUTH SIDE CANAL, NEAR TENTH STREET,

WASHINGTON, D. C.

---

mand of the Army of the Potomac and succeeded by General Burnside. 15th—Army of the Potomac commenced the march toward Fredericksburg. December 7th—Battle of Prairie Grove; rebel loss 3,000 killed and wounded; Union loss in killed, 167; wounded, 798; missing, 1,148. December 10th West Virginia admitted into the Union. 13th—Battle of Fredericksburg; Union losses 1,512 killed, 6,000 wounded, and 700 taken prisoners. 31st

box, as they have no conductor. This arrangement is very good, although we do not see why they should charge one cent more than the other lines. The White House is on Pennsylvania avenue, and is always open to visitors, although its occupant, the President, is not always to be seen. The

---

Battle of Murfreesboro ; rebels defeated ; 7,000 men lost in this fight, which lasted for six hours. January 1, 1863—The new year opened auspiciously for the Union arms : Missouri had been brought into subjection ; Kentucky, Middle and West Tennessee had been wrested from the rebels ; we had gained control of the Upper Mississippi ; Louisiana, the whole coast of North Carolina, and nearly all of South Carolina were ours ; also, the principal

grounds around the building are very pleasant. In the summer season there is music in front of the Mansion, and a great many of the citizens avail themselves of the opportunity to take a promenade through the grounds to see and be seen. The Marine Band, with their red coats, are always on

TALLMADGE & CO.

General Insurance Agency

373 D Street, between 7th and 8th Streets,

WASHINGTON, D. C.

REPRESENTING

Over $12,000,000 Capital

In the following old and favorite Companies:

UNION FIRE INSURANCE COMPANY OF NEW YORK AND SAN FRANCISCO, CAL. Assets $3,000,000.

GIRARD FIRE INSURANCE COMPANY OF PHILADELPHIA, PA. Assets $500,000.

FIREMAN'S FUND FIRE INSURANCE COMPANY OF SAN FRANCISCO AND NEW YORK. Assets $1,600,000.

First-class Solicitors can always find Employment at this Agency.
Insurance to any amount effected in first-class Companies.

seaport towns of Georgia, and our guns commanded the town and island of Galveston, Texas ; President Lincoln issued his emancipation proclamation. 19th $100,000,000 authorized to be raised to pay the army and navy ; the *Richmond Examiner* begins to predict the Southern confederacy a failure. 25th General Burnside relieved of the command of the Army of the Potomac, and was succeeded by Major General Joseph Hooker. March 20th

hand. and discourse fine music. An hour can be spent here very pleasantly.
Near by the Mansion are the War and Navy Departments. These buildings
are old, and insufficient in size to accommodate the business of the departments. The Government is about to build new ones, and very likely will

REMOVAL.

Dear Sir:
I take the liberty to inform you that I have removed my

MERCHANT TAILOR STORE

from opposite the Post Office to the

MARBLE BUILDING ON SEVENTH STREET,

OPPOSITE THE PATENT OFFICE,

Where I am now supplied with all the latest styles of Piece
Goods in the market, which I will make up in first-class
style, and at moderate prices.
 As I superintend the cutting in person, I consider it my
interest, as well as my customers', to see that no garment
leaves my store that is not entirely satisfactory.
 Hoping that my experience in business for the last four-
teen years; and having received a diploma of the first-class
at the Mechanics' Fair of 1857, is a sufficient guarantee that
I know something about the business: if so, a call is respect-
fully solicited.

FURNISHING GOODS

ALWAYS ON HAND.

JAMES LACKEY.

Battle of Milton, Tenn. 27th—Major General Burnside assumed command
of the Department of Ohio. April 7th—Attack on Charleston ; the gun-
boat fleet, under Admiral Dupont, made an attack on Fort Sumter, but after
an action of thirty minutes, in which several of the fleet were disabled, they
were compelled to withdraw ; in this action the rebels had 300 guns, while
the fleet had but 34. Ap. 29th—The Army of the Potomac commenced crossing

do so, if the capital is not removed to St. Louis, which mother rumor says is soon to take place. There are other departments of the Government that have not the necessary accommodations. The State Department, on Fourteenth street, is sadly deficient, and the White House itself is a disgrace to

J. W. SMITH,

ATTORNEY-AT-LAW

AND

Solicitor of Claims and Patents

Office, 254 F Street, bet. 13th and 14th,

WASHINGTON, D. C.

P. O. BOX 125.

HAVING resigned the position of Chief Clerk of the Second Comptroller's Office with a view to engaging in the practice of Law and the Collection of Claims against the United States, I respectfully solicit whatever business of that character the reader may have to transact at Washington.

For several years my business in the office of the Second Comptroller (whose functions are to decide finally on Army, Navy, Indian, and Pension Claims) has been to write decisions on the very points that are involved in the classes of claims I now propose to prosecute, and I must have improved my opportunities indifferently well if I have not obtained a more thorough and comprehensive knowledge of the laws and decisions governing such claims than other agents generally possess. It is the decision of the Comptroller that determines the fate of a claim—whatever may have been the action of the Auditor or administrative bureau—and persons interested will not therefore fail to see the advantage of entrusting, *especially large claims*, to one who is perfectly familiar with the practice and rulings of that office.

I will prosecute as effectually and promptly as the nature of the claims and of the public offices will permit, all claims growing out of breaches of contracts by the U. S.; or for rent of buildings or land; or for value or use of steamboats, houses or other property, taken or used by the Army or Navy; or for bounties, back pay, pensions and patents; also claims for the return of money improperly collected in the Customs or Internal Revenue Departments, as well as for the remission of fines, forfeitures and penalties.

No cases accepted that do not exceed $25, and no advance fee asked when I advise prosecution.

J. W. SMITH.

TREASURY DEPARTMENT, SECOND COMPTROLLER'S OFFICE.

Mr. J. W. SMITH, late Chief Clerk of this office, having resigned to engage in the business of his profession, I cordially commend him to the public. He is a gentleman of unusual acquirements, great industry, and spotless integrity, and intimately acquainted with the transaction of business in the executive departments. I feel pleasure in bearing this voluntary testimony to his character, after an official connection with him of several years.

J. M. BRODHEAD, *Comptroller*.

the Rappahannock; the rebel pickets were surprised, and 400 prisoners captured; 20 men wounded in the melee; the left wing, 35,000 strong, crossed four miles below Fredericksburg, engaged the rebels twelve hours, and drove them out of their rifle pits and a distance of eight miles. May 2 Battle of Chancellorsville; after three days' skirmishing the battle opened this afternoon; "Stonewall Jackson" was severely wounded in this fight;

the nation. You can reach the State Department by the New York avenue cars, that start at the junction of Fifteenth street and Pennsylvania avenue. The Art Gallery, on the corner of Pennsylvania avenue and Seventeenth street, is a fine building that is just opened to the public and to the lovers of

Grand Gulf captured by Admiral Porter and Gen. Grant : 500 prisoners, and a large quantity of stores taken. 14th Battle of Jackson : General Grant captured Jackson, Miss. : the State capitol was burned : the rebel Congress threatened to hang all commissioned officers of negro regiments who might fall into their hands : Gen. Grant defeated Generals Gregg and Walker at Mississippi Springs : Gen. McPherson occupied Clinton, Miss.

32

fine arts, and is a place of much interest. This building was presented to the city by Mr. Corcoran, and is a monument to his memory as a generous and noble gentleman, who preferred rather the public interest than himself. Washington may well be proud of such a benevolent citizen.

June 1st—Gen. Burnside suppressed the *Chicago Times* and prohibited the circulation of the *New York World* in his department; Gen. Kilpatrick reached Urbana, Va., from Yorktown; he captured on his raid over 500 horses and mules, 1,000 contrabands, and destroyed $2,000,000 worth of property. 5th—The Federals, in their operations, reached within speaking distance of the rebel works of Vicksburg; all the siege guns were opened.

The Observatory, situated on 21st street, will well pay the stranger to visit, as he will here find many things of interest. Like all departments of Government, this place is peculiar to itself, and helps to make up the great whole which makes Washington the most attractive city of the Union.

SHIRT MANUFACTORY.

Mrs. L. A. McLEAN,

OF NEW YORK,

(Who has had Twelve Year's experience in Troy, New York, and Phila.)

HAS ESTABLISHED HERSELF AT

No. 305 F Street, bet. 11th & 12th Sts.

WASHINGTON, D. C.

And is prepared to make, on short notice, and in the very best manner.

Gentlemen's, Ladies & Children's Underclothing

OF ALL DESCRIPTIONS.

ALL WORK WARRANTED.

PATRONAGE RESPECTFULLY SOLICITED.

and 3,600 shells were thrown into the city in one hour. 6th—John Ross, Chief of the Cherokees, offered President Lincoln a regiment, 1,200 strong, of loyal Indians. 8th—Gold in Richmond, 86 premium; silver, 85.50. 11th.—It is estimated at this date 50,000 colored soldiers have been enrolled into the United States service. 14th—Battle of Winchester. 15th—The President called for 100,000 men for six months. 27th—Gen. Mead suc-

The most beautiful and interesting park is Lafayette Square, situated on Pennsylvania avenue, between 15th and 17th streets. In the centre of this park is an equestrian statue of General Jackson, which is a fine work of art.

The Patent Office, situated on the corner of Seventh and F streets, is a

List of Prices
OF THE
HOWLAND DENTAL ASSOCIATION
No. 27 Four-and-a-half Street,
3d door north of Penna. Ave.

EXAMINATIONS AND ADVICE WITHOUT CHARGE.

Extractions under the influence of Nitro Oxide, without pain, first tooth..........$1.50
Each additional tooth, at same sitting... 1.00
Extractions without Gas, each tooth... .50
Administering Nitrous Oxide for operations of Felons, Tumors, Abscesses,
   and for Amputation and all minor and capital operations..... ....$1.50 to $5.00
   Hereafter no charge will be made for Extractions, either with or without Gas
where artificial teeth are inserted.
   Having greatly enlarged our facilities for performing Operative and Mechanical
Dentistry in all its branches, we are now prepared to do perfect work, warranted first
class, and to give entire satisfaction, at the following reasonable rates.
Gold Filling, ordinary cavities........ ....$1.00 to $5.00
Tin Filling, ordinary cavities.......... 1.00
Oseto-Dentine Fillings.. .75
Artificial teeth, full upper or lower sets... 20.00
Our temporary sets, when returned, will be replaced by permanent ones
   from...$3.00 to $7.50
   Root Filling and Regulating Teeth in proportion to our other operations.
   Dr. L. A. Strachan will be happy to see his friends and patients at the office of
the Howland Dental Association. Prof. Howland has now given the Nitrous Oxide
for dental and surgical operations to over fifteen thousand persons. See circulars or
testimonials at the office.

ceeded Gen. Hooker in command of the Army of the Potomac. 28th—Great excitement in Pennsylvania on account of the rebel invasion ; in Philadelphia all business suspended, and drilling took place. July 1st—Battle of Gettysburg, Pa. ; the fight was severe and attended with heavy loss ; Maj. Gen. Reynolds was mortally wounded ; the rebels repulsed, losing 6,000 prisoners ; the fight lasted three days ; the rebel loss was estimated at 2,439

department of Government that the visitor must see, for he will here find much to entertain him. It is from this wing of Government that the many documents best known as letters patent are issued ; and here will be found specimens of every article that has been patented since we have had a Gov-

---

Mrs. J. E. Spencer's

MILLINERY

AND

DRESS-MAKING ROOM,

330 Penna. Avenue, bet. 9th and 10th Sts.

LADIES

Who want Goods in my line will find a full assortment constantly on hand of the Latest Patterns, and prices as low as elsewhere in Washington.

CALL AND EXAMINE MY GOODS.

MRS. J. E. SPENCER.

---

killed, and 14,580 wounded ; the Union loss is set down at 14,000 killed and wounded : 20 battle-flags were taken by one corps ; flag of truce from Vicksburg, asking an armistice to arrange terms of capitulation ; Gen. Grant refused any other terms but those of an *unconditional surrender*, and thus it was done. July 4th—Battle of Helena, Ark. ; the battle was very severe, lasting six hours : rebel loss 1,500 killed and wounded, 1,130 prisoners, and

ernment. The building occupies two squares, and two entire floors devoted to models that have been patented. One must not go here expecting to look through this department in an hour, as days will be required to take any thing like an understanding view of the millions of different kinds of labor-

---

WILLIAM CAMMACK,

FLORIST,

Corner 13th and E Sts.

BOUQUETS,

CUT FLOWERS,

BASKETS OF FLOWERS,

WREATHS,

CROSSES,

ANCHORS, &c.

All persons stopping at the Hotels, by visiting me, or dropping me a line, can rely upon having their orders promptly executed in the neatest style of the Floral Art.

---

two pieces of artillery; Federal loss about 250. 6th 10,000 prisoners arrived in Baltimore from the Army of the Potomac; Lee retreated toward the Potomac, his army utterly routed, Mead in close pursuit. 7th—The fall of Vicksburg was announced to-day, and caused great rejoicing throughout the loyal States. 8th—Surrender of Port Hudson, Miss.; 5,500 prisoners, 2 steamers, 60 guns, 5,000 small-arms, 150,000 rounds of cartridges.

saving machines that the ingenuity of men have invented. First and most important to the inventor is the enriching of himself; but here is plainly proven that he has enriched the public, if not himself; for without the Yankee inventor it would seem impossible for society to exist. For example,

M. LOOMIS, M. D.

SURGEON DENTIST.

———◆———

All Styles of ARTIFICIAL TEETH made.

———◆———

TEETH FILLED MOST DURABLY,

AND WARRANTED.

———•••———

CHLORIC ETHER

(The only safe and reliable anæsthetic) skilfully administered.

•••

Dr. L. being the Inventor and Patentee of the Celebrated MINERAL PLATE style of Artificial Teeth, will make and adapt them to the mouth in the most perfect manner.

Office, No. 338 Pennsylvania Avenue,

NEAR THE CORNER OF NINTH STREET.

and 44,800 lbs. of cannon powder were captured. 9th—Morgan's raid upon Louisville : Lee still retreating toward Richmond, his army demoralized, and desertion frequent. 22d—Lee retreated to Winchester. 27th--Gold worth 1,100 per cent. premium in Richmond. 30th—Morgan captured, with McCluke and 28 others, and confined in the Ohio penitentiary. 31st--Gen. Burnside placed the State of Kentucky under martial law, believing the

what should we do to-day without the steam-engine, spinning-jenny, sewing machine, washing-machine, &c? You might as well ask a business man to take the old-fashioned stage coach to go from the far West to New York to buy goods, or undertake to supply New York with coal by pack-mules, as

---

BOOTS AND SHOES

ROBERT BALL,

491

7th Street, west side, bet. D and E Sts.

DEALER IN THE

Best and Cheapest

BOOTS AND SHOES OF EVERY STYLE

FRESH GOODS RECEIVED WEEKLY

FROM THE

Best Manufactories in New York, Philadelphia & Baltimore.

SPECIAL ATTENTION PAID TO

MAKING AND REPAIRING.

---

rebel raid was for the purpose of influencing the election on Aug. 3; the Union troops occupied Fredericksburg Heights. Aug. 1st President Lincoln issued a proclamation that he would retaliate in kind for any ill treatment of the Union soldiers, whether black or white, by the rebels; that the Federal uniform must be respected; desertions repeatedly occurring from Johnson's army; second siege of Charleston; the works on Morris Island

to attempt to do away with labor-saving machines such as are here found. To a patent-right man this department may be made especially profitable. as here may be found many improvements that have been patented and have not found their way before the public, either from the fact that the inventor

F. GERMUILLER,

Saddle, Harness, and Trunk Maker,

380 Seventh Street, between H and I,

WASHINGTON, D. C.

KEEPS CONSTANTLY ON HAND

Saddles, Harness, Trunks, Whips, Collars

AND EVERY OTHER ARTICLE IN HIS LINE OF BUSINESS,

ALL OF WHICH WILL BE SOLD

ON THE MOST REASONABLE TERMS.

N. B.—Old Saddles and Harness taken in Exchange for New; also, repaired at the shortest notice.

Persons at the hotels, wishing anything in our line of business, can be supplied at the shortest notice by dropping us a line.

---

silenced the rebel batteries. 3d—Gov. Seymour asked the President to suspend the draft in New York city, but was refused, and the draft proceeded through riotous times. 19th—Fort Sumter crumbling under the fire of Gilmore's batteries. 21st—Quantrell's raid into Kansas with 800 guerillas, firing the towns, and killing men, women and children indiscriminately; about 200 persons killed, and over $2,000,000 in property destroyed; Gen.

is too poor to introduce them, or lacks that Yankee go-ahead that is important to make even a good invention a financial success. The Patent Office, like all other Government departments, is furnished with a large library, which strangers can consult if they desire; and the librarian will be found a

Fashionable Dress-Maker.

MISS M. F. GORMAN,

Late of New York City,

HAS TAKEN ROOMS AT

500 Ninth St., bet. Penna. Ave. and D St.

WHERE SHE IS PREPARED TO DO

All kinds of Work in the above Line

IN

FIRST-CLASS STYLE,

And will guarantee satisfaction to her patrons.

Jas. H. Lane escaped on horseback, and rallying about 200 men, followed and fought Quantrell 12 miles south of Lawrence; Quantrell fled, closely pursued by the infuriated Kansans. 23d Gold in Richmond 1,600; greenbacks, 1,200. Sept. 4th Gen. Burnside occupied Knoxville, Tenn., amid great enthusiasm; bread riot in Mobile. 7th Gen. Gilmore occupied Fort Wagner; 75 men and 36 guns were taken. 13th President Lincoln, by

gentleman who will make those who visit him feel perfectly at home. The Post Office Department is one that needs but little said to make its use and interest known to the stranger; still, a few points may not be amiss, and a visit will pay one that has a few hours to spend. The dead-

HAMMACK'S
Restaurant,

Nos. 200 and 202 Penna. Avenue,

WASHINGTON, D. C.

BOARD AND ROOMS BY THE DAY OR WEEK.

MEALS AT ALL HOURS.

Best Wines and Liquors to be had at the Bar.

THOS. GREEN, Prop'r.

proclamation, suspended the writ of *habeas corpus* in cases of military arrests. 19th—Battle of. Chickamauga ; this continued two days with great slaughter ; Union loss, 1,644 killed, 9,262 wounded, 4,945 missing ; rebel reports place their loss at 16,499 killed and wounded, and 1,500 prisoners. Oct. 10th—Fight at Blue Springs, Tenn. ; the rebels, 6,000 strong, were defeated and driven from the field at sundown. 15th—Gen. Grant assumed

letter department is interesting. It is here that all letters that have failed to reach the place of their destination are sent and opened. If the writer's name can be learned, and his whereabouts, the letter is returned to him; if not, (and the letter is important,) it is put on file. Attached to the dead-

OAK HALL

Clothing House,

460 SEVENTH STREET,

Opposite Post Office.

command of the Military Division of the Mississippi, comprising the departments of the Ohio, Cumberland, and Tennessee, headquarters in the field. 17th—President Lincoln called for 300,000 more men, to be drafted Jan. 5th, if not sooner raised by volunteering. 24th—Maj. Gen. Butler ordered to the command of the 18th Army Corps, and the Department of Virginia and North Carolina, Gen. Foster being relieved. 25th—The rebels

letter department is a museum, created by the many articles that have been
sent by mail and found no owner. One will see here almost everything,
from a cambric needle up to a good sized engine. Hoopskirts, boots and
shoes, hats and caps, shirts, drawers, and stockings, birds, beasts, and

---

---

driven beyond the Sweetwater, Tenn. ; the fight was a desperate one ; rebel
loss over 300 ; Union loss nearly the same, and a battery of artillery ; at
Pine Bluff, Ark., 4,000 rebel cavalry, under Marmaduke and Cabal, attacked
Col. Clayton's command, 700 strong, but after a short fight were driven off,
losing 300 killed and wounded ; Union loss 11 killed and 33 wounded.
27th—Gen. W. T. Sherman appointed to command the Department and

snakes, hardware. jewelry. and medicine ; also pictures of dear ones enough to fill a country school house. In short. to enumerate what is not here would occupy much less space than to tell of the things that are. These goods are sold every few years to make room for more. Many hundred

---

Army of the Tennessee, and Gen. John A. Logan to command the 15th Army Corps; Shelby's guerillas driven out of Missouri ; three Greek-fire shells thrown into the centre of Charleston from the Morris Island batteries. 29th--The rebels attacked Gen. Hooker's position at Wauhatchie, near Lookout Mountain ; after two hours' severe fighting, they were repulsed and driven across Lookout creek ; Hooker lost 350 officers and men killed

clerks are employed in this building, as here is kept an account of all the different offices throughout the country. The visitor can form some idea of the magnitude of the business by looking through this enormous building. As a post office, this is not unlike many others that may be met with in

MRS. C. HOPPY,

RESTAURANT AND CONFECTIONER,

UNDER THE ST. CHARLES HOTEL,

Cor. of 3d St. and Penna. Ave.

Mrs. HOPPY keeps a full supply of

OYSTERS & FRUITS,

And will serve up

MEALS AT ALL HOURS,

IN THE FINEST STYLE, and

At Prices that will not fail to Give Satisfaction.

CALL AND TAKE A CIGAR.

46

other cities, as the same routine of business is transacted which is common to all postoffices throughout the country.

We will now take the visitor to the renowned Ford's Theatre, that is now occupied as a Medical Museum. It was here that Abraham Lincoln was

---

---

tle of Droop Mountain ; rebels defeated ; many rebels deserted during the fight. 7th The rebels attacked Gen. Burnside's outposts at Rogersville, Tenn., 60 miles from Knoxville, and captured 300 men of the 7th Ohio cavalry and 2d East Tennessee infantry and 4 guns, and retreated, fearing Gen. Shackleford, who was in the neighborhood ; rebel loss, 2 killed and 8 wounded ; Gen. Meade commenced his forward movement from Cedar Run ;

assassinated, since which time the Government has occupied it. Though somewhat changed, it is still the same place, and the spot may be seen on Tenth street as you pass down Pennsylvania avenue.

---

410 Pennsylvania Avenue,

Boots and Shoes Made to Order.

D. M. FURLONG,

THE GREAT ARTIST OF THE HUMAN FOOT,

Relieves Suffering Feet,

Warrants to Fit all kinds of Feet

Affected with Lumps, Corns and Bunions,

ON THE ANATOMICAL LASTS.

WARRANTED TO FIT AND PLEASE,

OR NO CHARGE IS MADE.

A TRIAL SOLICITED.

Anatomical Lasts made to order at Lowest Rates.

Warrants them to Suit

BEFORE BEING PAID FOR.

---

the 3d and 6th Corps crossed the Rappahannock at Rappahannock Station and Kelley's Ford, and after a spirited engagement took the rebel rifle pits and 480 prisoners and 600 Enfield rifles ; the rebels lost, besides, 100 killed and 300 wounded : Federal loss, 370 : over 1,900 prisoners. 4 guns, and 8 battle-flags were taken in this forward movement : the rebels destroyed the Memphis and Charleston railroad at Middletown.

LBJe79

www.ingramcontent.com/pod-product-compliance
Lightning Source LLC
Chambersburg PA
CBHW021643270326
41931CB00008B/1150